SUFFERING
WHILE SERVING

CONFRONTING HARD TRUTHS ABOUT
VOLUNTEERING IN MINISTRY

Written by Stephen Wingard
Editing by Dr. Tamarie Macon
Cover Design by Derrick Robbins
Layout Design by Adam Robinson

For permission requests, write to the publisher, at "Attention: Business Affairs," at the address below.

INSPIRE MEDIA LLC
430 East 162nd Street, Suite #545, South Holland, IL 60473
inspiremediabooks@gmail.com

Published 2017

Printed in the United States of America

Publisher: Inspire Media, LLC
ISBN: 978-0-9995089-0-9
ISBN (eBook): 978-0-9995089-1-6
Library of Congress Control Number: 2017916856

SUFFERING
WHILE SERVING

CONFRONTING HARD TRUTHS ABOUT
VOLUNTEERING IN MINISTRY

STEPHEN WINGARD

CONTENTS

SECTION 1

PERSONAL CHARACTERISTICS THAT LEAD TO SUFFERING

CHAPTER 1

THE SUFFERER

09

CHAPTER 2

THE MOTIVE BEHIND YOUR FRUSTRATION

22

CHAPTER 3

UNDERAPPRECIATED

30

CHAPTER 4

OVERWHELMING PERSONAL ISSUES

37

CHAPTER 5

HAVING AN AFFAIR ON YOUR FAMILY WITH THE CHURCH

45

PREFACE **01** REFERENCES **126**

SECTION 2

TEAM AND LEADERSHIP ISSUES THAT LEAD TO SUFFERING

CHAPTER 6

COMING TO GRIPS THAT SOMETHING IS WRONG   **57**

CHAPTER 7

UNHEALTHY CONTROL   **64**

CHAPTER 8

THE MOTIVATION FACTOR   **74**

CHAPTER 9

PERSONALITY DIFFERENCES   **81**

CHAPTER 10

MANIPULATION, VERBAL ABUSE, AND THE RESIDUE   **90**

CHAPTER 11

EXPOSING SIN   **102**

CHAPTER 12

WRONG LEADERSHIP   **113**

CHAPTER 13

SUFFERING = WINNING   **123**

The motivation for writing this book was based on the question:

Who supports the church volunteer dealing with emotional pain caused by those in leadership?

PREFACE

Life is complex and the challenges we face may appear to be unfair, but following God's course leads to wholeness! Many people pursue their own course, but stumble greatly because of their unwillingness to include Jesus in their journey. Life can still be challenging even with Him by our side. He told us it would be difficult as was His crucifixion. Despite His significance, suffering was required, a journey He could not avoid. Similar to a woman carrying a baby and later experiencing the pains from labor, we all will experience hard moments in life.

> When a woman gives birth, she has a hard time, there's no getting around it. But when the baby is born, there is joy in the birth. This new life in the world wipes out memory of the pain. The sadness you have right now is similar to that pain, but the coming joy is also similar. When I see you again, you'll be full of joy, and it will be a joy no one can rob from you. You'll no longer be so full of questions. This is what I want you to do: Ask the Father for whatever is in keeping with the things I've revealed to you. Ask in my name, according to my will, and he'll most certainly give it to you. Your joy will be a river overflowing its banks! (JOHN 16:21-24, THE MESSAGE)

01

Life can become overwhelming when balancing the demands of personal life responsibilities and volunteering. Things can become unstable and doubtful, but Jesus promises to return a similar measure of joy as a result of what we endure. In other words, the intensity of your pain will be similarly equal to the joy available from God. If you are presently suffering, God sees the state you are in. Your situation can change dramatically for your good! Jesus says He sees you now, but when He sees you later you will be restored with joy and no one will be able to take it away (John 16:23, MSG)!

The motivation for writing this book was based on the question: Who supports the church volunteer dealing with emotional pain caused by those in leadership? Thus, this book is helpful for those who attend Christian organizations and are reluctant to serve by way of volunteering. The work examines issues many people don't discuss while serving in Christian based organizations. Biblical applications are highlighted which are relevant to confronting issues in order to enhance teamwork and healthy leadership. The theme throughout is to identify common problems and propose solutions for resolving issues, all while encouraging volunteers to face conflict head-on.

Before placing blame on others, it's important to look inwardly first, which is why the first section identifies personal characteristics that can lead to suffering in ministry. Chapter one confronts the reality that many people are suffering but don't know how to confront the issues they face as volunteers; possibly

02

because many ministries intentionally or unintentionally disregard their pains. The second chapter examines the motive behind your frustration, as it is important to recognize your intention(s) for serving in ministry. Chapter three deals with feeling underappreciated, but emphasizes the importance of not seeking validation from man but from the Lord. This approach will help keep your motives intact God's way. Chapter four discusses overwhelming personal issues and how they can bring us closer to God if dealt with correctly. Even though God is fully aware of how we feel about our problems, it's important for our relationship with Him to convey our true feelings. This section ends with chapter five, "Having an Affair on Your Family with the Church." A common dilemma for families is balancing home-life and ministry responsibilities. This chapter emphasizes prioritizing correctly so that family is at the forefront.

Section two discusses broader topics that focus on team and leadership issues. If a ministry is composed of various parts (Praise & Worship Team, Media Team, Security), in order for it to thrive, each piece must constantly work towards enhancement and overcoming problematic areas. This section provides organizations with the tools needed to strive for excellence and growth.

Chapter six, "Coming to Grips That Something is Wrong," provides insight on recognizing when something is wrong within ministry. Addressing issues requires boldness and honesty. This chapter provides examples on how to correctly speak out when issues exist. Chapter seven defines unhealthy control, which can be displayed by those in leadership authority. Leaders can lead the wrong way, causing various problems, such as their people never adapting to perform independently or being unwilling to take risks because of micromanagement. Chapter eight discusses motivation and how it drives performance. Leaders have a responsibility to motivate and inspire. As volunteers serve with the intent to please God, leaders, in turn, must focus on creating excitement. As leaders do this, they can make serving attractive.

Chapter nine provides solutions for personality differences. No matter in or outside Christian organizations, when people work together, personality differences will exist because people are wired differently. This chapter brings attention to the importance of not being controlled by emotions when in uncomfortable situations. People may be unaware of how they come across, whether rude, irritating, or overall difficult to work with. We should push past our feelings and become intentional towards developing functional relationships with those we serve alongside.

Manipulation and verbal abuse are discussed in chapter ten. People model this negative behavior for various reasons, mainly to control others and hide their own insecurities. This should not be tolerated in any setting. God holds us accountable with properly addressing this issue in a healthy manner. We must follow God on the approach to take when addressing manipulation and verbal abuse. If we never separate

ourselves, essentially we choose to inflict ourselves by allowing others to abuse us.

Chapter eleven discusses the significance of exposing sin. No matter the type, it's important to correctly address sin when suspected within every Christian ministry. Do we all sin? Absolutely! Have people improperly confronted others suspected in sin and, as a result, caused extensive hurt? Yes. If ministries truly desire God's presence and blessings, they must make accountability the forefront for individual spiritual growth. The "don't judge me" ideology has plagued churches, lowering standards and compromising our morals. Exposing sin must be approached sensitively. Doing so requires boldness, a compassionate heart for people, and discernment of intentional and unintentional behavior. twelve The final chapter illuminate the blessing that comes when we endure suffering the way God intends.

Now, let's begin by identifying those who are frustrated in ministry but don't talk about it, the sufferer.

This writing is **NOT INTENDED** to discourage serving at Christian organizations. Instead, the motive is to produce **relevant approaches** that foster healing, growth, and success within church ministry and the personal lives of volunteers.

SECTION 1

Personal Characteristics that Lead to Suffering

CHAPTER 1

THE SUFFERER

Nicole is among other weary people, trying to relax and focus on the message preached this Sunday. All week she looked forward to this day because of constant irritations at home and being pulled in so many directions. For example, the volunteers who work in the nursery were getting shorter each month and no one else filled in the gap but her. This was her Sunday off. All she wanted was inspiration and hope poured into her because her personal life was unpredictable. Even though she's a dedicated church member, she hasn't enjoyed the benefits like others who come and go. Her mind is racing this day, thinking about if the nursery has enough coverage and she is becoming frustrated because in her mind, she is acting selfishly by not checking to see if there are enough volunteers this day.

In actuality, she was avoiding serving because two Sundays ago, someone said something inappropriate and she's still upset about it. Unable to focus, she then notices her director on the opposite side trying to make eye contact with her. They lock eyes and the leader signals with her mouth, "HELP," then gestures by swinging her arms rocking an imaginary baby. Nicole knew what this meant. She sighs, gathers her purse and other belongings, and heads to the nursery to serve.

The pastor stands before the congregation and says: "People in the Body of Christ are facing this new thing called 'church hurt.' They are leaving their churches and refusing to serve because of it." The pastor then challenges the people by asking, "What if someone on your job hurt you? Are you going to quit? We must move past 'church hurt' and learn to forgive."

In this scenario, the pastor is correct in acknowledging that people are more vocal today discussing their frustrations and hurts caused by the church. As a result of this, many are quitting church altogether, not necessarily abandoning God but choosing to isolate themselves from traditional worship gatherings. Are some people overly sensitive and more judgmental toward the church than anywhere else? Absolutely! Despite this, we cannot ignore real issues of abuse, manipulation, and deception prevalent in many ministries, especially when resources are tight and pressures are constant.

The pastor in the scenario is partially correct. We must mature, forgive, and develop useful ways of handling issues. But who holds the other party accountable as this is done? The difference between corporate jobs and serving in church is that if someone creates a hostile and uncomfortable work environment, Human Resources' (HR) responsibility is to ensure the situation is addressed. HR holds people accountable for sustaining comfortable work environments for employees. They support employees and protect the company.

10

THE SUFFERER

Who supports the church volunteer dealing with emotional pain caused by those in leadership or other volunteers?

What happens when serving becomes overbearing and putting on the fake smile is no longer tolerable? My answer is we must move beyond ignoring the issues that exist in the pews and stop using jargons like "just forgive" as a method to silence the real pain of those in need. Should we overlook issues while mistreatment and neglect continues? Leaders must stop comparing their church with companies when they have no organizational structure or culture for handling people responsibly. Unfortunately, some churches and ministry organizations are losing sight of the importance of taking care of people, in-house, those on the frontline serving. Like any other employer refusing to address issues, organizations risk losing quality people and jeopardize the reputation of their brand.

We must move beyond ignoring the issues that exist in the pews and stop using jargons like **"just forgive"** as a method to silence the real pain of those in need.

People who commit their time volunteering at a church or affiliated Christian ministry share many experiences with others, many of whom they may like, but some of whom they don't and wish they could speak their mind to. This, of course, would not lead to a positive outcome – even if it feels good in the moment. The reality is people can, and do, get on our nerves at some point! Working with others, especially believers (followers of Jesus), has its pros and cons, but overall, is very rewarding if done with pure intentions. It's a valuable commodity for any ministry if the focus is to transform lives and grow. You may have heard of small bible study groups later developing into thriving ministries able to impact communities, influence a city, and generate national attention. It's because of the people who serve, who willingly invest their efforts into some mission or vision that sparks motivation and sacrifice. These individuals have motivation to sacrifice even if it hurts them or the people around, but where is the balance with this? It's possible to serve in a capacity viewed as good or the mission of Christ on the front end, but their involvement could jeopardize personal relationships on the back end. This is a description of what Nicole is going through. Like so many, people keep giving and giving because in their mind, it's the right thing to do, but eventually what was supposed to be rewarding feels like extreme frustration and drainage. People are suffering while serving.

A common and easy out for people who feel they give more than they receive back is to continue frustrated (*even after addressing their concerns*) or to end the relationship(s) altogether. Whether on the job,

13

at school, or in the church, dealing with people can bring about complicated and uncomfortable situations. It's one thing to deal with drama on the job as employers pay you to suck-it-up. Family problems is another challenge as it's hard to avoid some relatives. When volunteering you have the freedom to walk away but serving in ministry is bigger than you! Even though the journey can be rough, serving should outweigh your inconveniences.

The ideal experience when serving is when everything is on your terms, constructed around your convenience(s), such as your schedule, or what you feel like doing, rather than going against your comfort-zone. Every growing and evolving ministry that you (may) volunteer at will require you to go beyond your comfort-level, beyond everything you initially intended when you signed up. As ministries grow, demand increases for talented, skilled, and excited volunteers with pure motives to serve. With growth, the demand on ministry resources increases as people from all walks of life gravitate to church assets. The church's most valuable asset, which must be well maintained, is having quality lay-workers, those who work voluntarily. America's most powerful and influential ministries are what they are today because of the constant support of volunteers.

If not carefully managed, "paid staff" can overshadow the significance of lay-workers. Individuals like myself who are involved in ministry experience all types of personal or ministry related issues. Money, health, family, issues on the job or with friends are circumstances we MUST not allow to negatively impact our attitude or deteriorate our motives for serving.

14

Every **growing** and **evolving** ministry that you volunteer at will require you to go **beyond your comfort-level, beyond everything you initially intended** when you signed up.

When problems arise, we look for an "out," a way to escape and experience relief. Pressures can become problematic when the pastor or others in leadership demand more from struggling volunteer(s). The usher, the children's ministry aid, the prayer warrior, and others are having issues but continue to project a smile as the pressures bombard them. On top of this, they may hear complaints from dissatisfied leaders barking on how more need to serve! The organization is selfishly complaining, minimizing and/or neglecting its responsibility to motivate. Volunteers must have leaders who are skilled communicators and who possess the passion to make ministry work attractive.

16

Then Jesus made a circuit of all the towns and villages. He taught in their meeting places, reported kingdom news, and healed their diseased bodies, healed their bruised and hurt lives. When he looked out over the crowds, his heart broke. So confused and aimless they were, like sheep with no shepherd. "What a huge harvest!" he said to his disciples. "How few workers! On your knees and pray for harvest hands!" (MATTHEW 9:36-38, THE MESSAGE)

Many people teach this passage from the perspective that Jesus was concerned with the harvest outweighing available and "fit" laborers, with which I agree. However, I saw this passage in another way as well. In verse 35, Jesus is curing and delivering people from all types of issues but in verse 36, he looked at the crowd and his heart was broken. If he just healed all the people, why is Jesus heartbroken? If he healed their bruised and hurt lives, where is His hurt stemming from? Is it possible he referred to a different group in the crowd? In verses 37-38, Jesus reveals a problem, not with those who were just healed, but with the laborers he instructed his disciples to pray for.

The laborers are the people who joined Jesus' mission, even while suffering with their own issues; they were attracted to the power and mercy Jesus demonstrated on the earth. These people were not near Him like the disciples, but nonetheless were a part of his movement – spreading the word of the supernatural man they encountered. Some of these individuals were viewed as the least likely to be delivered or set free from their bondages.

In Mark 5, the bible introduces a "madman" who lived in Gerasenes. This man was demonically possessed with major issues because he chose to live in a cemetery. The bible states in verses 3 - 4, "No one could restrain him – he couldn't be chained, couldn't be tied down. He had been tied up many times with chains and ropes, but he broke the chains, snapped the ropes. No one was strong enough to tame him. Night and day he roamed the graves and the hills, screaming out and slashing himself with sharp stones."

This "crazy cutter" was ultimately delivered from the "legions" he once was possessed by and soon afterwards, begs to travel with Jesus. "And when He had stepped into the boat, the man who had been controlled by the unclean spirits kept begging Him that he might be with Him. But Jesus refused to permit him, but said to him, Go home to your own [family and relatives and friends] and bring back word to them of how much the Lord has done for you, and [how He has] had sympathy for you *and* mercy on you" (Mark 5:18-19, Amplified).

Even though he was not allowed with Jesus, this man became a "laborer." He immediately became a Kingdom spokesperson who testified about the deliverance and break-through he experienced. "And he departed and began to publicly proclaim in Decapolis [the region of the ten cities] how much Jesus had done for him, and all the people were astonished and marveled" (Mark 5:20, Amplified). Does this sound like you? Were you – or are you – viewed as the least likely to come out of your situation with the ability to testify of God's redemption and grace on your life?

There are two examples of hurting people that God graciously redeems: the untamed man who lived in the cemetery cutting himself and the group Jesus became heart-broken for. Out of compassion, Jesus instructed his disciples to pray for them – the "harvest hands" in Matthew 9.

18

The demographic of those who feel overlooked continues today, yet **Jesus is sticking up for the hurting,** making intercession to the father on their behalf.

So, what do you think? With God on our side like this, how can we lose? If God didn't hesitate to put everything on the line for us, embracing our condition and exposing himself to the worst by sending his own Son, is there anything else he wouldn't gladly and freely do for us? And who would dare tangle with God by messing with one of God's chosen? Who would dare even to point a finger? The One who died for us – who was raised to life for us! – is in the presence of God at this very moment sticking up for us. (Romans 8:31-34 THE MESSAGE)

People may overlook you, but Jesus sees you in the crowd. Others may discount or give up on you like the crazy cutter from the cemetery, but God's grace and deliverance extends beyond opinionated limitations. If you are suffering while serving, He is heart-broken by your situation, and deliverance can be your portion!

20

KEY POINTS

- Serving in ministry is bigger than "you!" Even though the journey can be rough, serving should outweigh your inconveniences.

- Leaders must stop comparing their church with companies when they have no organizational structure or culture for handling people responsibly.

- Working with others has its pros and cons but overall, is very rewarding if done with pure intentions. It's a valuable commodity for any ministry if the focus is to transform lives and grow.

- People may overlook you, but Jesus sees you in the crowd. If you are suffering while serving, He is heart-broken by your situation, and deliverance can be your portion!

21

CHAPTER 2

THE MOTIVE BEHIND YOUR FRUSTRATION

When situations cause frustration, an immediate response is looking everywhere else other than yourself. When I was unemployed for several months, this was a frustrating period in my life as my wife and I were 3 years into our marriage and expecting our first child. Leading up to this, for years I had a strong desire to work for the Federal Aviation Administration (FAA). In my mind, a federal position was something prestigious.

For months, I spent hours completing long applications that required writing essays, but despite my persistence, I received no signs of interest from the FAA. It was during this time that I reconnected with a buddy I graduated with in college. Coincidentally, he worked for the FAA and frequently spoke on how much he liked his position. The hiring process for him was seamless. After he applied, they scheduled a phone interview and soon afterward, hired him without meeting him face-to-face. I wish I could admit I was happy for him, but frankly, I was mad and frustrated. I was mad with God and vented my frustrations towards my wife. In my heart, I deserved the same blessing this guy received!

> What is causing the quarrels and fights among you? Don't they come from the evil desires at war within you? You want what you don't have, so you scheme and kill to get it. You are jealous of what others have, but you can't get it, so you fight and wage war to take it away from them. Yet you don't have what you want because you don't ask God for it. (JAMES 4:1-2 NEW LIVING TRANSLATION)

I was guilty of committing sin in the 1st degree. I was coveting someone else's job. I wanted what he had and felt at a disadvantage. "No lusting after your neighbor's house—or wife or servant or maid or ox or donkey. Don't set your heart on anything that is your neighbor's" (Exodus 20:17, THE MESSAGE).

Why didn't they recognize my resume? We graduated from the same university, and I had more professional experience, so what was the problem? I spent the majority of my college experience serving in campus ministry so I felt I earned the job! These were my feelings and pride, ego, and covetousness were the motives behind my frustration.

It's important to understand the motive behind your frustration as this will determine the real problem. In my situation, the motive behind my frustration was the inability to relinquish what I believed I deserved. The covetousness in my heart regarding my buddy working for an organization I wanted to be a part of was why I was frustrated. Not getting

23

what I wanted and coveting someone else's possession was problematic and contributed to my frustrations. In order to determine if your frustrations are valid, you must consider the real issues that feed into your discomfort.

In professional fields, most people want to be recognized for good work. Problems can occur when positive recognition is not the result of hard work. This could condition a person to work with the motive of gaining recognition without exhibiting excellent performance. If they continue this approach eventually they will burnout and become frustrated. This is why it is important to assess the motive behind your frustration.

24

In ministry, you must always work with intention to love God's people. **Jesus never commanded you to like everyone, but He did require you to love and this should be your motive when serving.**

"For you were called to freedom, brothers. Only do not use your freedom as an opportunity for the flesh, but through love serve one another. For the whole law is fulfilled in one word: 'You shall love your neighbor as yourself'" (Galatians 5:13-14, English Standard Version). Consider love as your focus whenever involved with God's affairs.

Serving becomes tainted and out of the will of God when we do so with other intentions. If we serve without love, we will become deceived, thinking we are doing God and His people a favor. This can result in feeling despair and negatively used by people. People may believe their actions are right but fail to recognize they function with a wrong spirit.

"All the ways of a man are pure in his own eyes, but the Lord weighs the spirit" (Proverbs 16:2, English Standard Version).

26

If we serve without **LOVE,**

we will become **deceived,**

thinking we are doing God

and His people a favor.

What's the motive behind your frustration(s)? Are you serving to seek recognition or a higher position, but your efforts have failed you? Has this caused you frustration? Identify what your true intentions are. In most circumstances, if your motives are pure, you will encounter spiritual success. When an individual serves in ministry with impure motives, sin is lurking and will destroy.

"If you do well, will you not be accepted? And if you do not do well, sin is crouching at the door. Its desire is for you, but you must rule over it" (Genesis 4:7, English Standard Version).

When doing anything for the Lord and His people, you must constantly rule over the temptation of a "you scratch my back, I'll scratch yours" political approach towards ministry. This is a wrong mentality and you will fail at overcoming feeling frustrated or taken advantage of. I encourage you not to serve if this is your thinking because politics (in church) will eventually jeopardize relationships and your integrity when handling the affairs of God. This is why everything you do must come from a motive of love, compassion, and a desire to see God impact lives. If you approach serving God's Kingdom any other way, then disappointment, resentment, feeling taken advantage of, and a host of other negative emotions are inevitable. You serve because you love God, period! What's the motive behind your frustration?

28

KEY POINTS

- Identifying the root cause of your frustration will determine if your feelings are justifiable or wrong. This requires honesty and possibly the help of a mature believer who should evaluate your circumstances based on the Word of God.

- Your intentions for serving should be pure and because of the love of God and His people.

CHAPTER 3

UNDERAPPRECIATED

"What about what I've done?" "Did anyone notice me?" "Do 'they' even care?" These are common statements from those who feel underappreciated. Feeling valued is important in every relationship. Whether in marriage, working professionally, or in ministry, feeling appreciated is critical psychologically. If you were to place it on Maslow's hierarchy of needs, it would fit between "Love/belonging" and "Esteem." Abraham Maslow was an American psychologist who developed a theory for understanding human needs. Based on this, feeling underappreciated is a legitimate concern, but we must be honest and admit that some people can be extreme by throwing pity parties for themselves. Yes, humans need to feel validated, but it's important they receive it from a correct viewpoint.

> Whatever may be your task, work at it heartily (from the soul), as [something done] for the Lord and not for men, Knowing [with all certainty] that it is from the Lord [and not from men] that you will receive the inheritance which is your [real] reward. [The One Whom] you are actually serving [is] the Lord Christ (the Messiah). (COLOSSIANS 3:23-24, AMPLIFIED)

God acknowledges those who serve based on their intentions. The Lord acknowledged Job's intentions by describing him as a man blameless and upright (see Job 1:8). When serving, it's important to approach it with pure intentions. It's not about becoming popular or getting close to the pastor or any other leader. Serving should never be for networking purposes or doing it as a favor for someone else. The system of this world is totally different than the system of the Kingdom. As followers of Christ, we serve with the intention to "give." In the world, we serve or work with the intention to "get." This is where things can become complicated when trying to work the system of the Kingdom according to the laws of the world. These systems oppose each other and work according to different principles.

31

As followers of Christ, **we serve with the intention to "give."** In the world, we serve or work with the intention to "get."

No wonder some people feel underappreciated when serving. Their intent opposes how God wants us to approach servanthood. Some look to receive validation from "man" instead of the Word of God! It's interesting how God instructed us to approach every task, whether big or small. He wants us to operate passionately with the perspective of receiving directives from Him. Why? Maybe because He knows man is imperfect and does not know how people feel and receive appreciation. He knew eventually you would have to serve a boss, hard to please pastor, spouse, or child and He would want you to do it in love and with excellence! For this to happen, you would have to use your imagination with the perspective of serving as if it were Him however, this does not excuse leaders from their responsibility to motivate people.

Not all leaders possess the knowledge on how to make people feel appreciated. This is another reason why we must do everything unto the Lord. We should serve with the intent to give – period! The principle of sowing and reaping becomes activated once giving is set in motion. We should never focus on the benefits; doing so may reduce our blessing(s). The moment we do this, we restrict ourselves from receiving the hundred times return blessing.

As volunteers commit to God by serving and using their talents, **leaders** should, in turn, **focus on inspiring** and motivating those who serve.

We will dive more into this concept in chapter 8.

> Jesus said, Truly I tell you, there is no one who has given up and left house or brothers or sisters or mother or father or children or lands for My sake and for the Gospel's Who will not receive a *hundred times* as much now in this time—houses and brothers and sisters and mothers and children and lands, with persecutions – and in the age to come, eternal life. **(MARK 10:29-30, AMPLIFIED)**

Position yourself to be acknowledged by God just as he did Job. You do this based on your intentions for serving. With the correct perspective, you will never experience feeling underappreciated if you do everything unto the Lord. Feeling accepted and appreciated is a legitimate need but the bible never guaranteed you would receive this from man. Having the correct mindset will set you apart from others so "that you will receive the inheritance which is your [real] reward" (Colossians 3:24, Amplified).

35

KEY POINTS

- When serving, you should not seek validation from people because they are imperfect.

- Aiming to please people can cause major frustrations, as it may appear your sacrifices are never enough. Your work in ministry should be focused towards pleasing God.

- We have the responsibility to please God as we serve. Our leaders have the responsibility to motivate and make serving attractive.

CHAPTER 4

OVERWHELMING PERSONAL ISSUES

For some, hiding behind personal issues is an escape from reality. For others, it can be the most uncomfortable experience as they desperately seek freedom. The majority of us don't want people to know when we (ourselves) are dealing with hard-life situations. There could be several reasons for this. It could be our pride/ego of not wanting people feeling sorry for us, or possibly trust issues. When we haven't reached a level of trust with people and are dealing with problems, we act in self-preservation mode. When this occurs, a person can feel alone and without adequate support.

There was a period in my life while serving in ministry I dealt with financial lack. One day after returning from a 2-hour commute from work, I remember being tired and frustrated with my financial situation. I was underemployed with a wife and two children. This particular Wednesday, my wife wanted us to go to bible study. Upon arriving at church, I remember thinking, "I'm tired and don't have anything to pour out." At that time, I was involved with the prayer ministry and on this night, my pastor taught on the subject of prayer.

At the end of his message, he instructed the prayer team to come forward and assist those needing prayer in the congregation. I remember the moment clearly. I told the Lord, "I don't belong to myself, but I belong to You. I'm Your extension cord. Channel whatever it is Your people need from You, through me. I'm Your instrument." After my prayer, I put my emotions in check, prayed in the Spirit, and was ready to serve God's people.

Everything turned out great. God moved powerfully in my experience, which was rewarding. I remember leaving church, getting in my car, turning the ignition, seeing how low my fuel was and thinking, "I hope I make it home 'cause I don't have any gas money." I sighed and thought, "Well, back to reality." My frustration returned immediately.

At that moment I realized when you activate prayer, you take yourself away to function in the spirit with God – a dimension greater than the natural. I was dealing with the effects of coming back to earth; coming back to my circumstances which ministry allowed me to escape from.

You can only hide so long until the feeling of being burdened becomes overwhelming. Some of us even play God or act as though we can hide our true feelings from Him. In our relationships with people, there are times when we won't reveal our true feelings because of fear of separation. We all do this at some point in our lives either towards our spouse, boss, and

38

even God. I was an expert at doing this. I was frustrated with life and felt cheated by God. Even though I felt this way, I didn't DARE share this to God while in prayer. I respected and feared Him too much.

One day while in my kitchen, my heart was heavy as I worried about life. I responded the way church trains you in those moments. I started to pray and began to praise and tell God how wonderful He was to me, but then I stopped. In that moment, I felt so fake as though I was lying to God's face. I then said, "Lord, I'm frustrated and mad with you right now!" I immediately heard the voice of God speak so clearly, "Now we're ready to begin!" He revealed in that moment it was time to get real, stop faking, and see firsthand Him "work everything together for my good" and deliver me one victory at a time.

At that moment, I instantly became free from a relational barrier that prevented me from going boldly before God's throne of grace and I obtained the mercy and help I needed (Hebrews 4:16). It felt as though a glass barrier had shattered, a barrier symbolizing separation and fear. I now understood that God would not be upset and reject me because of my straightforwardness. Jesus is not about religion but relationship, yet religion had conditioned me to avoid truth. I felt one way but told God something else with my mouth, which made me a liar. This is God, the One who is described as knowing every strand of hair on my head (Matthew 10:30).

Being real or respectfully honest towards Him can bring about healing and a greater level of closeness.

39

After reaching this place with the Lord, my circumstances changed, having experienced one small victory after another.

> Likewise the Spirit helps us in our weakness. For we do not know what to pray for as we ought, but the Spirit himself intercedes for us with groanings too deep for words. And he who searches hearts knows what is the mind of the Spirit, because the Spirit intercedes for the saints according to the will of God. And we know that for those who love God all things work together for good, for those who are called according to his purpose. (**ROMANS 8:26-28, ENGLISH STANDARD VERSION**)

If we love the Lord with our whole heart, something good is coming forth as a result of suffering while serving Him. Sometimes when in a battle, there's nothing more you can do but endure until the end. One day as I was walking and listening the voice of God pertaining to a dilemma in my life, I asked the Lord, "Lord, give me a solution to this problem. What else can I do?" His response was, "There's nothing you can do; just endure!"

Like most addicts (e.g., alcoholic, workaholic, technology indulger) people can use "ministry" to escape from life circumstances. Some use it as a drug to hide from home-life realities. Of course we need mental breaks to think on things other than our problems, but it's important not to become so dependent on ministry that we neglect life outside of church. It's also easy to become so engulfed in the ministries

40

we serve that we develop a fear of facing personal problems.

When church is over for the day, marital, health and/or financial issues wait at home for many of us and because of this, we are suffering. While facing our issues, we must learn how to endure hardships, but this can only happen if we have a correct view of serving. I created the following motto, which motivates me when I don't feel like serving: "If I give myself to serve, I will be made to endure." What this means is the byproduct of serving is developing the endurance needed to overcome any obstacle. This is vital in life! Based on this logic, managing a lifestyle of serving will develop your strength for overcoming problems, even some we placed ourselves in.

Let's go back to Nicole from chapter 1. *While she is passionate about serving in the nursery ministry, she is overburdened* with an emotionally absent and possibly cheating husband. His priorities are work and taking advantage of available overtime. When away from his job, he prefers video games and friends because he feels his schedule conflicts with Nicole's. This is one of the reasons she feels the only time he communicates is when initiating sex. This isn't working for Nicole because she's tired of the same ol' and communicates this, but he feels what can he do about his schedule?

There are many predicaments we put ourselves in because of poor choices and decisions. There are other life-situations that surprise us, but can help develop certain qualities we need to take us to our "next level" of maturity.

41

Strangely as it sounds, overwhelming personal issues can bring us closer to God in the end. We must fear the Lord from a biblical stance and confidently reveal our heart to Him, even though He already knows its condition. Lastly, sometimes the Lord will reveal an exit strategy for our issues, while other times we have to trust and persevere. No matter the situation, in the end, we as believers have the tools to win!

42

KEY POINTS

- When suffering from overwhelming circumstances, it's important to be honest with God and voice your true feelings to Him. He already knows how you feel, but He desires you to freely express these concerns with Him.

- Jesus is most concerned about your openness with Him.

- It's important not to hide your problems by serving, pretending they don't exist.

43

For some of us, our involvement with church responsibilities has distracted us to the point **we can't hear the cry of help from our loved ones** who desparately need our attention to save them.

CHAPTER 5

HAVING AN AFFAIR ON YOUR FAMILY WITH THE CHURCH

When you're preoccupied with yourself, it's likely you'll neglect the responsibility to sustain healthy relationships with family and the people close to you. This may be because we are conditioned to believe family should be loyal and have our back, even when we are in the wrong. When family relationships deteriorate, some of us believe their loyalty to us should always hold firm. This is especially true when people outside our family attack our relatives. Ask feuding siblings how they would react if someone outside were to inflict harm on their brother or sister. In most cases, the response would be they would defend the other, despite the condition of their relationship with their sibling, all because of love. This holds true in most situations, but love requires people to be intentional.

Most men are intentional with making sure they earn the most, whether it is respect, money, or overall security. Because women are wired differently from men, they are intentional in other areas such as loving their significant other, caring for their children, and anything else in which relationship is the driving force. These differences can be problematic when serving in ministry especially for married couples.

When researching facts to support this chapter, I was presented with mixed opinions concerning Jesus's position on family responsibility versus His expectations for developing disciples (new followers of Him). On the surface, there appears to be a fight between managing both roles. Let's examine scripture:

> And it occurred that as they were going along the road, a man said to Him, Lord, I will follow You wherever you go. And Jesus told him, Foxes have lurking holes and the birds of the air have roosts *and* nests, but the Son of Man has no place to lay His head. And He said to another, Become My disciple, side with My party, and accompany Me! But he replied, *Lord*, permit me to first go and bury (await the death of) my father. But Jesus said to him, Allow the dead to bury their own dead; but as for you, go *and* publish abroad throughout all regions the kingdom of God. Another also said, I will follow You, Lord, *and* become Your disciple *and* side with Your party; but let me first say good-bye to those at my home. Jesus said to him, No one who puts his hand to the plow and looks back [to the things behind] is fit for the kingdom of God. (**LUKE 9:57-62, AMPLIFIED**)

46

In this passage, Man #1 informed Jesus he would go wherever He went. From a practical sense, Jesus's response was, if you follow after me, your Hotel

Reward benefits or frequent flyer perks might not help you in the places I send you. Jesus said, Foxes have lurking holes (*makes hunting easy*) and birds have nests, but the Son of Man has no place to lay His head. In other words, Jesus was saying some days He may minister in the Hamptons (NY), while on other days, He may be in the ghettos of Chicago, Detroit, or Compton (CA). The lesson here is, ministry may not always cater to your personal comfort standards.

Moving forward in the passage, Jesus invites Man #2 to accompany Him as a disciple. When the invitation is extended, the man makes a request to bury his father. Jesus surprisingly responds, "Allow the dead to bury their own dead; but as for you, go and publish abroad throughout all regions the kingdom of God." This could immediately be perceived as Jesus being insensitive, but I believe He was speaking more so of a spiritual death. Jesus's comment, "allow the 'dead' to bury…" gives this notation. How could Jesus respond so abruptly when His father (God) commands us to honor our mother and father? I believe the big picture God wants us to see is the value of time and the importance of not wasting it.

Finally, Man #3 tells Jesus he will follow him and become his disciple, but first needed to say good-bye to those at his home. Jesus responds saying, "No one who puts his hand to the plow and looks back [to the things behind] is fit for the kingdom of God." Based on the context of Jesus's response, I believe Jesus is warning us about the importance of not looking back at our shortcomings. If Jesus were speaking of family,

47

this scripture would mean we are against God if we do not forsake our spouses and children for the Gospel. This is clearly not the case. Jesus is referring to our secret shortcomings. We keep our issues and problems hidden away at home where no one can see. The lesson in this passage is if we are truly pursuing Christ, we must stay focused on what's ahead of us and forget about things we've repented from. What's interesting about these passages is that they (all) refer to family versus following Jesus. It's important to understand the points Jesus is making and what following Him may entail. We must review our responsibility toward our families from a biblical stance.

> If anyone wants to provide leadership in the church, good! But there are preconditions: A leader must be well-thought-of, committed to his wife, cool and collected, accessible, and hospitable. He must know what he's talking about, not be overfond of wine, not pushy but gentle, not thin-skinned, not money-hungry. He must handle his own affairs well, attentive to his own children and having their respect. For if someone is unable to handle his own affairs, how can he take care of God's church? (1 **TIMOTHY 3:1-5, THE MESSAGE**)

48

Those who God has assigned as spiritual authorities in our lives must model biblical standards for others to follow. The bible is clear that those in authority are an example to others.

> Remember your leaders *and* superiors in authority [for it was they] who brought to you the Word of God. Observe attentively *and* consider their manner of living (the outcome of their well-spent lives) and imitate their faith (their conviction that God exists and is the Creator and Ruler of all things, the Provider and Bestower of eternal salvation through Christ, and their leaning of the entire human personality of God in absolute trust and confidence in His power, wisdom, and goodness). (HEBREWS 13:7, AMPLIFIED)

With that said, this scripture is applicable to everyone, not just those seeking to be a Bishop or any other church leader.

If God requires us to be committed to our spouse, accessible, and hospitable, we cannot allow our family to become causalities for the sake of the Gospel! Paul is clearly against this belief in 1 Timothy 3, speaking specifically about our relationship with our children. He states we should be attentive to our children and have their respect. An emotionally absent mother or father is not regarded as providing necessary attention and garnering respect from a child.

> Husbands, go all out in your love for your wives, exactly as Christ did for the church – a love marked by giving, not getting. (EPHESIANS 5:25, THE MESSAGE)

How can a husband obey this biblical standard for marriage if he's constantly away from home, involved (attention toward) with people other than his wife? He will be unable to provide the same sacrifices as Christ did for the church, which involved dying. Jesus died for the church, meaning He offered Himself. It's impossible to "offer" yourself to your wife when you've already given yourself away. What you'll be doing is giving your wife seconds, thirds, and possibly fourths after others have already received the best parts of you.

> Wives, understand and support your husbands in ways that show your support for Christ. (**EPHESIANS 5:22, THE MESSAGE**)

50

It's difficult for a woman to support a man she views as selfish. Actually, it's difficult for ANYONE to tolerate a selfish person. Selfish people don't last long together because they put themselves before others and healthy long-lasting relationships require giving.

People differ, especially men and women. Women are natural receivers and require emotional care. Because of this need, if they don't receive it, their significant other may come across as selfish or insensitive. Men must understand that women possess unique emotional needs. They must regularly serve and pour into their wives and daughters emotionally.

Because all women are not the same, men must adapt and provide the level of love and emotional support God wired for her to receive. Maybe this is why Paul instructs married women to "understand."

To simplify the concept of women being "understanding," let's summarize it this way: After courtship, engagement, and saying "I do," women must recognize it can take time for a husband to provide the essential emotional care she needs. This emotional care is different than what was needed to win her over. The care I'm describing is what's needed to sustain and grow a healthy marriage because the reality is that after marriage, most people change! Men need time to adapt. This is not to justify men being relationally lazy, as many unfortunately are. In most cases, women are very gifted to understand their husbands quicker than men are when trying to understand their wives. Based on scripture, women must provide the same grace they would extend Jesus towards their husband. With this said, if women are devoted to ministry work more than their husbands, this prevents his ability to learn his wife. Again, the same attention a woman would give Jesus is what is required for her husband, according to the bible.

Imagine a grown adult male living with his disabled mother. The son has no job and lives off of disability insurance because of his mother's condition. He spends the majority of his day playing video games while his mother struggles to care for herself and provide living necessities. Every day her health deteriorates due to household responsibilities like cleaning, mowing the lawn, and random maintenance work. These actions are extremely strenuous to her body. One day she collapses in the kitchen but the fall is drowned out by video games projected from the son's

50-inch television rental. The mother lies on the floor, calling her son's name but he can't hear his mother's cry for help.

For some of us, our involvement with church responsibilities has distracted us to the point we can't hear the cry of help from our loved ones who need our attention to save them. Similar to loud video games, church is our entertainment and may be a major distraction from family priorities. Disappointingly, our attention is focused on people outside our homes, yet we return from ministering to the world and relax within our broken families. Some have become so accustomed to this, they don't (A) recognize anything is wrong and (B) feel inadequate when it comes to ministering to loved ones.

Servanthood is important, but it should first start at home. Imagine a funeral and the people most affected are those other than the deceased's immediate family – the reason being that the family felt the person in the casket was deceased from their lives years earlier. This is a scenario I hope is troubling. When we don't balance ministry and our home-life, not only will we suffer, but also the individuals who should be the first to benefit from our serving.

52

KEY POINTS

- Ministry may not always cater to your comfortable standards.

- If involved in ministry, it will require sacrifices such as being okay if you are not always accommodated AND focusing on how the needs of your family are best met.

- If you neglect the needs of your family, not only will they suffer, but eventually you will also.

- Servanthood should start at home. Your family should not receive you as seconds or thirds after you've given others the best part of you.

SECTION 2

Team and Leadership Issues that Lead to Suffering

CHAPTER 6

COMING TO GRIPS THAT SOMETHING IS WRONG

During the 2009 economic downturn, I worked at a transportation company. The effects of that recession caused financial problems for many companies across the US and my company was no exception. Management needed to eliminate a position and I was at the bottom in terms of seniority. Thankfully I had a general manager who recognized my value and decided not to terminate my employment, but instead temporarily transferred me to another department until the necessary revenue was regained.

I started work in the new department excited. I was ready to embrace my new role with new teammates whom I did not know prior to the transfer. After two weeks, I noticed major problems.

Even though my General Manager called this group a "team," they did not function as one. The most recognizable member worked horribly with people. Her interaction with others was demeaning. People who worked around her were intimidated because of her influence with management and some believed she had the power to get others fired if they crossed her or if she didn't like them.

Because I value teamwork, I was faced with a serious problem. Should this dysfunctional group continue as it was so that the success it was achieving would not be compromised? Something was wrong! This group was seriously divided. I was lost in the crowd not knowing what to do because of how others ignored her dysfunctional actions. I was left questioning if something was actually wrong.

When there are unaddressed issues within a group, if not careful, participants can develop a dysfunctional culture that in their mind is normal. They become numb to the problems that exist and conform to unhealthy relationships. Communication suffers and the group will deteriorate. Participants may use statements such as, "This is how we are" and use other excuses for chaos because they have become conditioned to it.

A concern for anyone experiencing unhealthy teamwork is when they fail to recognize a problem is present. As extreme as it may sound, this is similar to an addict denying s/he has a sickness. When it comes to facing problems within ministry, we usually give people the benefit of the doubt. New believers especially may have difficulty accepting that conflict exists because of the misconception that all Christians act lovingly and approach problems responsibly.

In Paul's writing to the church of Corinth regarding his third visit, he ended the letter with these instructions: "And that's about it, friends. Be cheerful. Keep things in good repair. Keep your spirits up. Think in harmony. Be agreeable. Do all that, and the

58

God of love and peace will be with you for sure. Greet one another with a holy embrace. All the brothers and sisters here say hello" (2 Corinthians 13:11-13, THE MESSAGE).

Before we as believers can "Think in harmony" or "Be agreeable" we must accept the reality that we all have flaws, which vary based on how we communicate. All of these issues should be addressed. Salvation is a similar action where we must come to grips and accept the fact that we were once (or are) dead in sin and need Jesus. This same principle must be applied if you suspect you are suffering while serving in ministry. Understand that Jesus requires us to walk in love, but also in that walk, we have to confront personality flaws among people. Come to grips that Christians aren't perfect, and if there are issues, this is a part of the Christian journey. How you function and, most importantly, how you respond in a difficult journey is an indicator of your personal development. We will explore personality differences more in chapter 9.

When there are **unaddressed issues within a group,** if not careful, participants can develop a dysfunctional culture that in their mind is normal. **They become numb** to the problems that exist and conform to unhealthy relationships.

In regards to the difficult situation on my job, it wasn't until people from other departments started noticing the tension on my team when I decided I had to confront the co-worker. Not surprisingly, I did not get along with this individual and people around us saw the tension between us. I was fed up with the ways she disrespected others and the team as a whole. Because she was successful at what she did, she gave the impression she could treat people however she felt. I decided to have a sit-down meeting with Human Resources so my concerns could be heard fairly.

The end result of my predicament is that this woman never changed. Despite this, I'm confident my decision to approach the women proved to my boss, HR, and the people around that I had pure intentions. Those intentions were to ensure my team was healthy and I was willing to speak out. Realizing something was wrong and change was needed gave me the confidence to appropriately address the issues. This individual ended up resigning from the company on bad terms years later, but to a few, I was recognized as the person who was not intimidated and would not tolerate foolishness. After I came to grips that something was wrong, I took a stand, attempting to stop communication madness and help turn my team around.

So what if you're frustrated because of specific circumstances – do you see the big picture? Can you admit and accept that something is wrong? Many people are frustrated with a lot of things but fail to come to grips with the truth! Are you covering up

61

any issues or failing to recognize what's causing your problem(s)? If so, you'll continue the cycle of being frustrated unless you realize problems exist and you may be the spokesperson needed to speak out. Come to grips!

62

KEY POINTS

- It's important to embrace truth when problems exist within ministry.

- When people ignore issues, pretending they don't exist, they will suffer from frustration.

- We must make attempts to work in harmony with one another in ministry. When doing this, we must accept that we all have personality flaws.

CHAPTER 7

UNHEALTHY CONTROL

At the time of writing this chapter, my oldest daughter will be turning 4 in two days. Looking back, fatherhood has been the most transformative experience of my life. My oldest, Sarai, amazes me each day with the 1,000 + questions regarding anything that catches her attention. As parents, my wife and I serve her in many capacities, particularly as leaders. We intend to impart the same moral principles as "Jesus followers" and hope to develop our daughters into healthy and successful decision-makers. If our goal is to be effective leaders to our children (which it is), we must be careful not to control them in an unhealthy manner, which could paralyze them from making sound decisions.   An interesting characteristic about Sarai is she is very selective about her attire. At times, she and I bump heads regarding what I want her to wear versus what she wants. There was a situation when I wanted her wearing her UGG (brand) boots while she wanted her Kenneth Cole's (brand). I am guilty of using my authority as her leader and have controlled her into wearing what I want her to wear without listening to her opinion. My wife pulled me aside one day when Sarai and I had our usual attire "drama episode" and informed me that not giving Sarai the opportunity to think creatively will hurt her development with making decisions. If I didn't change my approach and give Sarai shoe options, Sarai could end up being a ten-year-old unable to pick out her own shoes. One day I took my wife's advice and allowed Sarai to pick out her shoes. I remember her saying, "Daddy, I don't want to wear my UGG boots because they hurt my feet." After hearing this, I was in total shock. For so long I never gave her the opportunity to explain why she didn't want to wear these boots. I was so concerned with her matching and getting season wear out of the boots. I was unhealthily controlling my daughter by making her wear boots that were too small for her.

Many leaders aren't listening to volunteers who have solutions to problems that exist. Volunteers who are passionate about ministry are voicing their opinions about programs that don't fit or are no longer effective. Just like Sarai, they are ignored even though they possess solutions to problems their leaders may not know exist because they (volunteers) experience them first-hand. As already mentioned, I wanted Sarai to get the most season wear out of her boots. Similarly, leaders want the most use from programs, which they should, but problems develop when these programs don't fit the needs of the people.

> As for the one who is weak in faith, welcome him, but not to quarrel over opinions. One person believes he may eat anything, while the weak person eats only vegetables. Let not the one who eats despise the one who abstains, and let not the one

who abstains pass judgment on the one who eats, for God has welcomed him. Who are you to pass judgment on the servant of another? It is before his own master that he stands or falls. And he will be upheld, for the Lord is able to make him stand.
(ROMANS 14:1-4, ENGLISH STANDARD VERSION)

A problem at many ministries is the unwillingness of leaders to embrace individuals with different perspectives, those not intimidated to "go against the grain." A reality for most leaders is they prefer "yes men" – people who agree with them in most cases. These people unfortunately build a "bubble" around the leader in which there is disconnect between what the leader wants versus what's needed. Conversely, many leaders groom their staff to conform into "yes men" by their leadership style, which is usually prideful and egocentric.

66

Now you [collectively] are Christ's body and [individually] you are members of it, each part severally *and* distinct [each with his own place and function].
(1 CORINTHIANS 12:27, AMPLIFIED)

Whether on the job or serving people in pews, we all are pieces to one puzzle. No matter the size, each puzzle piece is valuable. When volunteers are not valued, they may experience a sense of containment. They may feel their ability to develop individually is restricted because of the unhealthy "system" they volunteer within.

As Paul mentions in Romans 14, we must welcome believers who don't see things the way we do. This means leaders should encourage opposing viewpoints regarding ministry. Problems occur when leaders create a culture where those who oppose the leader's ideas are ridiculed or in some places, demonized. Some volunteers may feel they are disrespecting their leader or acting in rebellion if they oppose opinions from pastors or head leaders. What's important is their approach when voicing their opinions. I once heard a pastor say that he pays people to disagree with him. This is part of his church's success.

In order for leaders to effectively develop their people, they must create a culture where people feel comfortable expressing bad ideas. Many times, people are afraid to contribute their ideas because of unhealthy responses from others. But bad ideas usually leads to discovering good ideas. Of course it should never be someone's intentions to express bad ideas when planning ministry related projects, but if people are comfortable enough, the most effective ideas can come from these forums.

I spoke earlier on how I have used my authority against Sarai for control purposes so that she agreed to what I wanted her to wear. Many leaders in the church use this same tactic for getting people to agree to what they want. Because they are in authority, some don't listen to the opinions of those they supervise and lead. In my example with Sarai, I was controlling her by having her wear boots I wanted her to wear while ignoring her attempts to communicate

67

that they were too small and were hurting her. Abuse is a strong word, so I would describe my actions as neglecting to hear a valid issue from my daughter. I was teaching her that she had no opinion, and if she did, it wasn't good enough. I was blocking her development as a decision-maker and similarly, this is what many leaders are doing with church staff. They have unhealthy control and the people around them are prevented from making decisions on their own.

I remember going away on a business trip with my VP of sales. At dinner, I asked her questions about her leadership style and the overall production from the people she managed. She was upfront in stating that her people got along and worked well with each other, but lacked taking the initiative when she is not around. When presented with issues, they always freeze, and looked to her for answers. This had me wondering if her leadership abilities were negatively affecting her team.

Many encounter similar performance issues like this, but the person who should be held most accountable is the leader. Is it possible when issues develop, leaders take unhealthy control by relinquishing responsibility away from their people? Is it possible leaders could have people in place they don't trust or feel are incompetent and their actions show this? Maybe staff members are coming up with solutions but their superiors reject them because they want things done "their way." No wonder people are frustrated – leaders are cultivating a "one man / woman show," yet they complain they have no support! When

68

problems occur, instead of immediately blaming others, leaders must look at themselves.

> "Do not judge others, and you will not be judged. For you will be treated as you treat others. The standard you use in judging is the standard by which you will be judged. "And why worry about a speck in your friend's eye when you have a log in your own? How can you think of saying to your friend, 'Let me help you get rid of that speck in your eye,' when you can't see past the log in your own eye? Hypocrite! First get rid of the log in your own eye; then you will see well enough to deal with the speck in your friend's eye. (**MATTHEW 7:1-5, NEW LIVING TRANSLATION**)

When individuals on a team feel unvalued or don't have ownership, they will always look to others. Most people in these circumstances won't waste their time volunteering because of the many obstacles that prevent healthy teamwork and communication. The outcome from this could result in large ministries with limited volunteer help.

Volunteers must feel they are valued and be given ownership over responsibilities without it being taken away. Similar to my example of Sarai picking her shoes, eventually I needed to give her this responsibility or else she would always be dependent on me. As her leader, I needed to listen to her in order to recognize the "real" issue for her not wanting to wear the boots I wanted her to wear. When leaders fail to listen to their people, their organization will suffer.

The volunteers who work on the front-line possess solutions to existing problems, but these individuals will be prevented from making responsible decisions when opportunities arise when leaders exhibit unhealthy control.

When leaders are presented with opposing viewpoints from volunteer staff, they must be open and address different opinions positively. Even though pastors or other ministry heads may make final decisions, they must cultivate an environment where people are free to openly express ideas. It's important to have a level of freedom so that if bad ideas are presented, people don't feel judged or ridiculed.

70

A problem at many ministries is the unwillingness of leaders to **embrace individuals with different perspectives,** those not intimidated to "go against the grain." A reality for most leaders is they prefer "yes men" - people who agree with them in most cases.

In most cases, how people function on a team is a reflection of their leadership. Leaders set the tone and create the culture on a team, so when people are struggling, usually there is an issue with leadership. Leaders are like gardeners. Based on their personality and intentions, they have the authority over what should be developed or weeded out from their team. It is important for people to be managed so that their personal skills are enhanced and later on, future leaders are developed. In order to produce the right people, with the right attitude and skills, leaders must establish the "right" environment for people to grow within. A free environment with open communication is vital! Leaders, it's not about you! It's about how you develop the people who serve so that they become a better leader than you! This is effective and unselfish leadership.

72

KEY POINTS

- Many leaders today aren't intentionally listening to volunteers who have solutions to the problems that exist within their organization.

- Leaders must embrace different perspectives and those willing to disagree with their ideas. The "yes crowd" will cause major problems within ministries and organizations.

- When volunteers are not valued, they may experience a sense of containment. They may feel their ability to develop individually is restricted because of the unhealthy "system" they volunteer within.

CHAPTER 8

THE MOTIVATION FACTOR

Many Christian affiliated organizations deteriorate when they refuse to manage their resources (finances & people) with a business model and professional approach. Many shy away from this, but the reality is "business" is an activity incorporated in all relationships, not just in corporate offices. It's an everyday feature of our lives. Just because our Christian focus is "winning souls" does not mean we neglect implementing the same behaviors and processes used on our jobs when volunteering or leading in the church. Business helps people meet objectives and establishes beneficial relationships. In order to do this effectively, people must be motivated.

A church cannot afford to pay every person who signs their name on a volunteer sign-up sheet. This is why you must effectively keep volunteers engaged to a vision. If churches and ministries hope to attract and keep volunteers, leaders must possess the skill to motivate. Volunteers should serve with the intent to please God, not man. On the opposite side, leaders should serve with the focus to motivate in order to achieve excellence, because of their love for God's people. If leaders fail at motivating, it will be hard to maintain consistent volunteer participation.

If churches and ministries hope to **attract and keep volunteers**, leaders must possess the **skill to motivate.**

Families today, more than before, are comprised of both parents working to support their household. Unfortunately in single-parent families, especially those with lower incomes, people have busy schedules that restrict their freedom and ability to serve. Those who do serve and are committed at their church might face challenges stemming from lack of motivation. No matter the circumstances, if lay-workers show a lack of enthusiasm, leaders must address this immediately and bring excitement to serving. Effective leaders are wired to motivate while impactful volunteers desire to please God with their efforts. Their focus is God and not pleasing man. This should be a continuous cycle and if it doesn't exist where you serve, I encourage you to change the culture.

Leaders must inspire people. It's not about badgering people with scriptures that highlight the importance of servanthood. Yes, Jesus is the supreme example of one who served, who laid down his life and because of this, we should serve. People agree with this point, but still need more from leadership to keep them engaged once (if) they decide to follow the example of Christ in regards to serving. They need positivity and motivation!

Even though corporations compensate for performance, some still don't understand the correlation between motivation, initiative to develop people, and the effects on employee skill level. Wilson & Madsen (2008) referenced Myers (1970) by stating, "'Skill level is not wholly independent of motivation. In fact, to a certain extent, it is dependent upon motivation.' He added that when the development of employees is not actively promoted by an organization, employee motivation and skill level are neglected" (p.6). This concept should also be applied to the church. When ministries neglect to develop paid and unpaid staff, motivation and skill level are affected.

Even though some churches do not apply that concept, the "world" is so deceptively appealing that some have applied negative worldly concepts and have incorporated it into their ministry. For example, they use extrinsic motivation methods in attempts to control – believing it's for the good. Pastors, Deacons, Church Boards, and others purposely manipulate people, thinking it's justifiable for the cause of Jesus. Wilson & Madsen (2008) stated the following:

"These types of rewards and reinforcements can be positive or negative. Reinforcements that encourage desired behavior are positive while those that punish undesired behavior are negative. Managers have tended to draw upon extrinsic factors such as salary, job security, working conditions, promotion, termination and demotion to motivate employees to learn new skills. These extrinsic rewards and treats are limiting, transitory, and can even create antagonism between employee and manager" (p.5).

An unfortunate situation is when there is tension between leadership and staff workers. Issues remain unresolved because of minimum communication between both parties. Instead of supporting each other, both groups have trust issues and are quick to blame and find fault with the other. This is why Christian ministries need successful and enthusiastic leaders who know how to keep people engaged and remain committed.

If leaders want influence, they must **gain the trust of people** and convince them **to believe in themselves**.

Study any successful leader and you will notice their ability to encourage people is what sets them apart. Their skill to make people believe in themselves is what enhances their influence with people. If leaders want influence, they must gain the trust of people and convince them to believe in themselves. They can do this through their ability to motivate. When people are motivated and focused on a vision, this will spark a movement for change and a mission will be fulfilled. So if you are a leader who prays that the mission at your church will be carried out, focused on those who support the mission by building them up through motivation.

KEY POINTS

- No matter the circumstances, if lay-workers show a lack of enthusiasm, leaders must address this immediately and bring excitement to serving.

- Effective leaders are wired to motivate while impactful volunteers desire to please God with their efforts.

80

CHAPTER 9

PERSONALITY DIFFERENCES

"Side-eye" looks and sighs of disgust are a few reactions from those who experience personality differences with others. We all have encountered some degree of discomfort or annoyance towards someone. Things can become very complicated when we experience this in ministry.

As followers of Jesus, we're expected to have positive attitudes and act "appropriately" according to God's Word. This holds true especially when involved in ministry. We must be honest with ourselves and admit that certain traits in people annoy us. Whether it's the way they convey their thoughts, how they joke, or how they express their opinion, certain traits can "rub" us the wrong way. It's ridiculous for others to demonize those who have these experiences.

I have personally experienced interacting with someone whose personality conflicted with mine while in ministry. The individual was my small group leader and after a month working with her, her presence irked me. This may sound harsh, unkind, and possibly unsaved, but my leader annoyed my Type A personality!

The leader constantly directed attention toward herself and talked the most during group discussions. This behavior occurred during teleconference calls and in-person. I found casual conversations very odd and when she joked, in most cases, I didn't relate and was not humored. Working with her on top of having to submit to her leadership was a disaster, but I pulled through.

Like my situation, interacting with someone whose personality doesn't sync well with yours can be challenging. This can cause many to become annoyed and uninterested in putting extra effort into a relationship outside of church. Like me, you may find casual conversations uncomfortable because of personality preferences you've always held on to. How do you overcome this obstacle?

You may wrestle with the thought: "The devil put this person in my life to frustrate me." The truth is we won't be "best of buddies" with everyone we interact with and that's okay. It is our responsibility to refrain from isolating or neglecting people and display love despite differences.

Many people get involved in ministries with impure motives and this can negatively affect others. Conversely, there are individuals who are very passionate about ministry, but struggle balancing conversations and activities connected to their passions. For example, if someone has a heart for children's ministry, they likely enjoy talking about related topics. Their passion gravitates them to anything associated with children's ministry. When someone is flowing in

82

their area of expertise, they feel personal fulfillment and a sense of purpose. This is why we must exercise our discernment to determine if someone is acting selfishly or simply struggling to control their enthusiasm and balance conversations connected to their passions.

We should constantly seek opportunities that will improve our personality traits. We should also keep in mind that there are individuals who are unaware of how they come across. These individuals may not have people in their life providing feedback on their personality flaws. This is why accountability is important, which requires us to go beyond how we feel in order to help someone else.

It is our responsibility to refrain from isolating or neglecting people and **display love despite differences.**

> "If a fellow believer hurts you, go and tell him —
> work it out between the two of you. If he listens,
> you've made a friend. If he won't listen, take one or
> two others along so that the presence of witnesses
> will keep things honest, and try again." (**MATTHEW
> 18:15-16, MSG**)

Problems can develop within any group when there are unaddressed issues. We won't be able to fix every situation, but the bible holds us responsible to reach out to those we have conflicts with. Notice the scripture does not say to get the opinion of others to determine if they share the same concerns. This is an automatic response because when we are frustrated we want immediate validation. The issue with this is what if the individual or people you discuss the issue(s) with don't share the same concerns but mention other areas. Your frustration most likely will increase. This then produces a toxic situation called "gossip" which destroys character and credibility.

Feeling annoyed or frustrated because of someone's personality is okay. **How you respond** when annoyed **is an indicator of your maturity in God.**

The scripture states, "work it out between the two of you." Don't jeopardize your character or others' by involving people in your personal matter. Others may not carry your same concern(s). If they do, you all should help fix the problem before others notice or become frustrated. When working within any team, it is your responsibility to help improve or correct behavior that does not enhance teamwork or bring about progress.

It's important to be truthful and admit to yourself if personality differences exist between you and someone else. If you are a follower of Jesus Christ, don't feel demonized just because someone else may irritate you. God wired us differently and there is purpose for this. Feeling annoyed or frustrated because of someone's personality is okay. How you respond when annoyed is an indicator of your maturity in God. God holds you accountable to respond appropriately despite how you feel. He wants you guided by the Holy Spirit and not by your frustrations.

87

> But the fruit of the [Holy] Spirit [the work which His presence within accomplishes] is love, joy (gladness), peace, patience (an even temper, forbearance), kindness, goodness (benevolence), faithfulness, Gentleness (meekness, humility), self-control (self-restraint, continence). Against such things there is no law [that can bring a charge]. And those who belong to Christ Jesus (the Messiah) have crucified the flesh (the godless human nature) with its passions and appetites *and* desires. If we live by the [Holy] Spirit, let us also walk by the Spirit.

[If by the Holy Spirit we have our life in God, let us go forward walking in line, our conduct controlled by the Spirit.] Let us not become vainglorious *and* self-conceited, competitive *and* challenging *and* provoking *and* irritating to one another, envying *and* being jealous of one another. (**GALATIANS 5:22-26, AMPLIFIED**)

If we belong to God, we must develop the skill to crucify our flesh when we feel the need to gossip or act on our emotions. Our flesh is composed of passions, appetites, and desires. Our conduct must be controlled by the Spirit. The bible never says we won't feel or experience certain frustrations and emotions that come with life. We should never condemn ourselves or others because of "feelings." Feeling annoyed, irritated, or angry is not an indication of our spiritual maturity. For people to say we shouldn't "feel" a certain way is unbiblical as God gave us emotions to manage and process. We come from different families with socio-economic backgrounds which have influences. These influences vary and shape who we are. How we respond in our actions when faced with these emotions is the key to our success. So what's controlling you?

88

KEY POINTS

- We must be honest with ourselves and admit that certain traits in people do annoy us.

- The truth is we won't be "best of buddies" with everyone we interact with and that's okay. It is our responsibility to reframe from isolating or neglecting people and display love despite differences.

- You should not jeopardize your character by gossiping about others who may be unaware of their personality issue(s). How can you help the problem instead of building separation?

89

CHAPTER 10

MANIPULATION, VERBAL ABUSE, AND THE RESIDUE

When managing people, various approaches can be used which typically are based on the leader's personality. There are advantages and disadvantages to different approaches, but the way an individual interacts with others is a reflection of their character.

Many people lead based on their observation of others. Those who look to become leaders usually gravitate to specific styles and approaches that get people responding how they want. The problem with this is when we come across manipulative and abusive practices.

Unfortunately, manipulation has a unique influence on people. Some leaders use manipulation as a tactic to get people to respond how they want, especially in organizations that rely heavily on volunteers. Sadly, the church is not exempt from this practice. Many Christian organizations can't afford to pay all of their staff workers. Once compensation is excluded for services, it can become difficult for leaders to obtain commitments from people and inspire them to work with excellence. This is why many resort to the use of manipulation.

For [you seem readily to endure it] if a man comes and preaches another Jesus than the One we preached, or if you receive a different spirit from the [Spirit] you [once] received or a different gospel from the one you [then] received *and* welcomed; you tolerate [all that] well enough! Yet I consider myself as in no way inferior to these [precious] extra-super [false] apostles. But even if [I am] unskilled in speaking, yet [I am] not [unskilled] in knowledge [I know what I am talking about]; we have made this evident to you in all things. But did I perhaps make a mistake *and* do you a wrong in debasing and cheapening myself so that you might be exalted *and* enriched in dignity *and* honor *and* happiness by preaching God's Gospel without expense to you? Other churches I have robbed by accepting [more than their share of] support for my ministry [from them in order] to serve you. And when I was with you and ran short financially, I did not burden any [of you], for what I lacked was abundantly made up by the brethren who came from Macedonia. So I kept myself from being burdensome to you in any way, and will continue to keep [myself from being so]. (**2 CORINTHIANS 11:4-9, AMPLIFIED**)

How many times have you "cheapened" yourself because of the use of manipulation? In this passage, Paul informs Corinth they were deceived, and realizes his mistake committed against Macedonia. Corinth welcomed erroneous teachings, which were leading people away from Jesus. These false teachings were welcomed and taught by eloquent speaking hot shot speakers. Paul noticed Corinth's response and how engaged they were and as a result, decided to serve for free, at the expense of other believers from Macedonia. The Amplified bible highlights it this way:

> Other churches I have robbed by accepting [more than their share of] support for my ministry [from them in order] to serve you. And when I was with you and ran short financially, I did not burden any [of you], for what I lacked was abundantly made up by the brethren who came from Macedonia. So I kept myself from being burdensome to you in any way, and will continue to keep [myself from being so]. (**2 CORINTHIANS 11:8-9, AMPLIFIED**)

The presence of manipulation causes a demonic ripple effect. The false teachers started this cycle by corrupting and seducing Corinth. Corinth welcomed these teachings and the cycle continued with Paul compromising the financial strength of his ministry and possibly his reputation with Macedonia as they paid more, having to provide more resources when Paul's expenses were Corinth's responsibility.

Manipulation must be exposed and immediately driven out of any organization if it intends to have a thriving culture. It's similar to a virus that spreads and will deteriorate an organization's reputation. Organizations will have difficulty attracting and retaining volunteers due to lack of trust with leadership.

Manipulation in the church may be comprised of the use of deception and lies in order to control people. It can compromise relationships and jeopardize an organization's ability to thrive operationally. The use of manipulation is broad and many have experienced it, especially the use of verbal abuse.

92

Manipulation must be exposed and immediately driven out of any organization if it intends to have a **thriving culture.**

Verbal abuse is the intentional or unintentional use of language to intimidate, control, or inflict psychological distress. According to ("Having Words: Verbal abuse in the Workplace," 2001): "Unlike physical violence, verbal abuse is still viewed in some quarters as a 'reasonable' occupational hazard for employees" (p. 37). Viewing verbal abuse as "reasonable" within any context is problematic. Some people justify this behavior especially when leaders are under stress or experience certain pressures.

When someone is verbally abused (either as an isolated occurrence or continuously), the wounds can be traumatic. Ask any person who has encountered this type of abuse; they most likely will confirm that the effects can carry over into other relationships. Unfortunately, verbal abuse occurs within some Christian organizations, leaving people hurt, confused, and suffering while serving.

I have personal experience with verbal abuse while volunteering. The organization I was involved with was hosting an event and guests had to be shuttled by buses. I was designated to help and was responsible for loading and facilitating transportation. While on the bus, I had to act as the group's motivator, getting people excited for the event. Once my group was loaded, we waited for further instructions as other buses were being loaded.

Communications were vague and plans for the event were put in place at the last minute, making everyone unsure of what to do and when to go. While waiting, my leader was walking by our bus and screamed onboard, "WHO'S IN CHARGE OF THIS BUS?" I answered, "I am." Then they responded in an aggressively aggravated tone, "WHY ISN'T THIS BUS MOVING?" Shocked and embarrassed by the confrontation, I nervously responded, "I'm waiting on the bus in front of us to load so we can follow." The leader then responded angrily, "THIS WAS NOT YOUR INSTRUCTIONS. WHY ARE YOU WAITING ON THEM WHEN YOU SHOULD BE DIRECTING THIS BUS? GET THIS BUS MOVING!" The leader stormed away leaving everyone puzzled and most likely glad they weren't in my shoes.

Because of my leader's action, I was humiliated and wanted to leave the event, but I couldn't. This wasn't any regular leader; this was a mentor who had verbally abused me in front of a group of fifty people. I still had to motivate the people while deeply hurting and confused over my leader's blunt reaction. It was one of the most uncomfortable and hurtful experiences of my life. If someone else had spoken to me in that manner, I would have reacted differently, but this was a leader whom I respected.

I never mentioned how hurt I was by the situation to my leader because God directed me NOT to. This was a completely different approach than the idea that whenever you have a problem, you should privately confront the issue. How else will people know if or when they are in the wrong? God wanted to deal with me first and have me address issues within my heart. I had to exhibit turning the other cheek, which

95

was against my Type A personality but was necessary in order for God to produce healing in my heart. By following the direction of Holy Spirit, my own issues – which included intimidation, fear, and pride – were addressed. Had I ignored God's leading, I would have responded out of my pain and embarrassment, reacting with the intent to win an argument that I was right.

When in conflict, most people (with the exception of those who prefer physical altercation) seek to be heard. While this is important, many overlook the big picture. People can talk at each other and accomplish nothing. This is why it is important to follow God's leading so that you end up healed and whole instead of feeling bitter and broken. There are situations when God releases you to address conflict head-on and other times when you may have to keep quiet and allow God to work things out for your good. In my situation, I kept quiet, examined my heart, and saw God work things out for my good.

96

In situations when God instructs you to turn the other cheek, He wants to handle the situation more effectively than you! This may be one of the reasons the bible says vengeance is the Lord's.

> Dear friends, never take revenge. Leave that to the righteous anger of God. For the Scriptures say, "I will take revenge; I will pay them back," says the Lord. (ROMANS 12:19, NEW LIVING TRANSLATION)

People can talk **at each other** and accomplish nothing.

Again, when abuse is present, it may require addressing the issue yourself (with God's leading) OR examining your heart (with God's leading). No matter the action, a response is needed.

No one should be a victim of verbal abuse, whether in a marriage, professionally, or while volunteering. The residue from it is traumatic and can be long-lasting. Several studies (as cited in Jacobs, 2005) have found that victims of workplace violence, which does not exempt verbal abuse, suffered related effects including "short and long-term psychological trauma; fear of returning to work; changes in relationships with co-workers and family; feelings of incompetence; guilt; powerlessness; fear of criticism by supervisors or managers; diminishing self-confidence; social isolation; lower job-satisfaction and organizational commitment; difficulty concentrating; difficulty remembering information; elevated levels of tiredness; unsafe behaviors; increased propensity for accidents and poor lifestyles habits" (p.45).

Verbal abuse should be approached objectively. Those who work for any organization, for pay or voluntarily, should never comprise their emotional well-being by tolerating this behavior. God always requires one response when you are subjected to abuse: seeking His guidance on how to address the issue. This may require confronting the issue head-on with the individual(s) OR opening your heart and allowing God to expose any hidden issues within your heart which must first be addressed. I dealt with my abuse obeying the voice of God and because of this, my emotional state is now healthy. I confronted the issue the way God led me to address it. Again, not all confrontations require you specifically facing the abuser. Depending on the extent of the abuse, it may require outside intervention, up to and including the police or legal counsel involvement. With God's leading, your reaction may require walking away and separating yourself (short-term or long-term) from the dysfunctional and unhealthy relationship.

With addressing abuse, you must position yourself on a successful path. God has the ability to direct your journey towards healing and freedom from abuse if you consult and give Him ALL the broken pieces of your heart.

> Lean on, trust in, *and* be confident in the Lord with all your heart *and* mind and do not rely on your own insight or understanding. In all your ways know, recognize, *and* acknowledge Him, and He will direct *and* make straight *and* plain your paths.
> **(PROVERBS 3:5-6, AMPLIFIED)**

99

When any form of abuse occurs, the victim should consider all options available to remove themselves to avoid additional trauma or occurrences. Some victims become incapable of doing this due to the trauma which impairs sound judgment. The negative effects of abuse occur immediately. According to Jacobs (2005), "the moments that immediately follow a traumatic incident of workplace violence are characterized by shock, a sense of disbelief and physical-psychological numbing" (p. 45).

The usage of manipulation and verbal abuse has affected relationships for centuries. Many leaders have developed their leadership styles based on their personality and how they saw others lead. There are positive and negative consequences with this as people strive to influence others. Leaders look to various methods to influence and many times it (unfortunately) involves manipulating people to produce the results they need. This is why it's important to take immediate action which must first be seeking God's direction. We must be guided by the Holy Spirit on how to appropriately confront this issue. It may include confronting the person directly or separating yourself altogether. There are circumstances when walking away is more effective than verbally confronting someone privately. Again, it's important to be led by the Holy Spirit. No matter how you confront the issue (as long as it's Godly), the use of manipulation and verbal abuse must stop!

100

KEY POINTS

- The presence of manipulation causes a demonic ripple effect.

- Manipulation must be exposed and immediately driven out of any organization if it intends to have a thriving culture.

- God always requires one response when you are subjected to abuse: seeking His guidance on how to address the issue. This may require confronting the issue head-on with the individual(s) OR opening your heart and allowing God to expose any hidden issues within your heart which must first be addressed.

- With addressing abuse, you must position yourself on a successful path. God has the ability to direct your journey towards healing and freedom from abuse if you consult and give Him ALL the broken pieces of your heart.

101

CHAPTER 11

EXPOSING SIN

SHHH! Don't tell! It's no surprise that churches and other organizations hide information from the public when staff members are involved in sin and other immoral behaviors. It's important to approach these situations responsibly once someone is suspected to be involved in such behaviors. The problem occurs when the individual continues in ministry and his/her sin is unaddressed because of the absence of true accountability.

Hidden sin has caused major problems for centuries. Biblical evidence shows that unaddressed sin produces devastating consequences. David's adulterous cover-up for sleeping and impregnating another man's (Uriah) wife (Bathsheba) later destroyed his family. By secretly murdering Bathsheba's husband and their marriage, his affair displeased the Lord and caused the following family issues:

- David's child with Bathsheba was struck with an illness and consequently died.
- David's daughter Tamar was raped by her brother Amnon.
- David's son Absalom killed Amnon for raping Tamar.
- Absalom turned against David by raping his concubines and seeking to kill him.

When ministries fail to address sin, the people who serve will suffer because **the standard for Godly morals and integrity will diminish.**

These are some of the consequences that occurred because of David's actions. Based on this, it is evident sin destroys, especially his family.

For years, the "don't judge me" perspective has plagued Christian organizations to the point that accountability is nonexistent. The reason for this may be that the church has altered its position from one extreme to another. Christians used to judge the mistakes of others so harshly that they pushed them away from the church and God. As a result, the church was not a safe place to be transparent and reveal your struggles. Once revelation on grace was taught, a transition occurred and the church became more comfortable for unbelievers.

As the exposure of popular Christian figures caught in sinful lifestyles circulated, a change occurred. To protect their leaders, some churches justified immoral behaviors and in doing so, this created a domino effect of compromise. Some churches confuse the usage of grace when they should be removing people from ministry altogether who are involved in sin. Unfortunately, this is where some organizations have ended up, ignoring their responsibility to properly address issues head-on.

When ministries fail to address sin, the people who serve will suffer because the standard for Godly morals and integrity will diminish. As a result, an organization's reputation may suffer and God will eventually remove his presence UNLESS efforts are made for correction. Those who serve with pure intentions for God but are under these ministries

104

should have a problem when sin is not addressed. They should fear God instead of man and therefore should vocalize their concerns. Again, problems arise when we don't know when to apply extending grace and when to sit someone down in ministry.

Romans 5:18-20 highlights the significance of Grace. The New International Version sums it up as "where sin increased, grace increased all the more."

> Here it is in a nutshell: Just as one person did it wrong and got us in all this trouble with sin and death, another person did it right and got us out of it. But more than just getting us out of trouble, he got us into life! One man said no to God and put many people in the wrong; one man said yes to God and put many in the right. All that passing laws against sin did was produce more lawbreakers. But sin didn't, and doesn't, have a chance in competition with the aggressive forgiveness we call *grace*. (**ROMANS 5:18-20, THE MESSAGE**)

> So what do we do? Keep on sinning so God can keep on forgiving? I should hope not! If we've left the country where sin is sovereign, how can we still live in our old house there? Or didn't you realize we packed up and left there for good? (**ROMANS 6:1-2, THE MESSAGE**)

105

Romans 6:1-2 helps us understand that God's unlimited grace is connected to our intentions towards sin. If a person struggles in an area but does not make consistent efforts to correct their behavior, their actions show they are choosing to live defeated.

Grace is unlimited, but God judges based on your intentions for making changes. This is why accountability is vital and will help people thrive in their relationship with Christ.

An accurate biblical approach for "judging" is misunderstood possibly because of worldly influence and societal norms. Another reason may be because of misapplication of scripture pertaining to this topic and not viewing this issue in the correct context. As mentioned, some churches have moved from one extreme to another and as a result, people are confused and living carelessly. I was conflicted with this until God introduced the concept of "accountability through grace."

Some of us are guilty of finding fault in others, ripping them apart, and missing the importance of restoring them back to life! Maybe because of how we saw others deal harshly with people, we follow the same unloving trend, brutalizing those with issues and then using the excuse of holding people accountable. With accountability, we MUST remember to operate with grace. This involves correcting one another so that we are in-line with God's standards, AND while doing so, display grace and bring restoration so that people are built up instead of torn down. How would you want someone to approach you if your sin was exposed? We must remind them that yes, they missed the mark and are wrong, but they can recover and live the life God wants them to live because of His grace! You restoring the person back to "life" should outweigh your critique.

106

> Brothers, if anyone is caught in any transgression, you who are spiritual should restore him in a spirit of gentleness. Keep watch on yourself, lest you too be tempted. Bear one another's burdens, and so fulfill the law of Christ. For if anyone thinks he is something, when he is nothing, he deceives himself. But let each one test his own work, and then his reason to boast will be in himself alone and not in his neighbor.
>
> For each will have to bear his own load. (GALATIANS 6:1-5, ENGLISH STANDARD VERSION)

When you discover or suspect another believer serving in ministry is involved in sin, this can be very uncomfortable. The higher the person is in leadership, the more intimidating it can be to address the issue. Because of the "don't judge me" philosophy, many shy away and will continue to serve alongside those they know to be in sin. This produces hypocrisy and unhealthy environments for effective ministry.

Contrary to popular belief, the Apostle Paul instructed us to confront sin among believers:

> I can hardly believe the report about the sexual immorality going on among you—something that even pagans don't do. I am told that a man in your church is living in sin with his stepmother. You are so proud of yourselves, but you should be mourning in sorrow and shame. And you should remove this man from your fellowship. Even though I am not with you in person, I am with you in the Spirit. And as though I were there, I have already passed judgment on this man in the name of the Lord

> Jesus. You must call a meeting of the church. I will be present with you in spirit, and so will the power of our Lord Jesus. Then you must throw this man out and hand him over to Satan so that his sinful nature will be destroyed and he himself will be saved on the day the Lord returns (1 **CORINTHIANS 5:1-5, NEW LIVING TRANSLATION**)

When I initially studied this scripture, I thought Paul was specifically speaking on the importance of confronting those in sin. Upon further study, I realized Paul is actually bringing attention to those in leadership who are desensitized, unwilling to recognize the issue, and who look the other way when sin is exposed. Essentially, when we pretend sin is not present, we are condoning the behavior. The Corinthians didn't love the people enough to steer them back on course. They had a twisted view of grace which meant they purposely developed a tolerance for sin. The focus is not on addressing the sinner, but the leader who tolerates it.

Paul states in this passage that when sin is present within a church family, it should break people's hearts. It should bother those in ministry when someone serving is involved in sin. We shouldn't look the other way, acting as though it will disappear on its own. We must take action and address it with grace or we will continue to have heavy hearts.

I remember when my wife and I moved to Chicago after college, we met a couple that was engaged to each other. We participated in a spiritual development class together at our church. One time while on a double dinner date with them, we discovered the couple was already living together prior to marriage. This information surprised my wife and me because one moment we were talking about the deep things of God and the next, this couple spoke of living together as though nothing was wrong with it. They were clearly involved in blatant sin.

This situation bothered me because as his brother in Christ, he needed to know he was disrespecting his fiancé by living with her. He was crossing boundaries God did not intend for him to cross while unmarried. I wrestled with the thought of having the conversation with him because I didn't know how he would respond. I couldn't shake the fact that this was not okay according to God's standards and knew I was obligated as his brother to confront the issue.

After the confrontation, surprisingly he responded positively, but asked if I was uncomfortable with him living with his fiancé. He didn't understand that I had nothing to do with how he lived his life. He wasn't living his life to please me, but God. His life-style was equivalent to someone owning and operating a vehicle without a license, which is illegal according to law. I wanted them to live blessed and favored but this could not happen according to God's principles.

The couple continued living together and a child came about. They got married but not even six months later, they separated because the boyfriend suspected his fiancé of cheating and wanted a paternity test. This situation continued to spiral downward and several months later I saw him with another woman.

When there is disagreement among people, understanding personality types and the level of the relationship (e.g., Friends, Spouses, or just Acquaintances) are determining factors with how successful addressing conflict will be. For instance, a married couple who individually have aggressive personalities might have issues during any type of confrontation. Let's say the wife is frustrated with her husband's decisions with money. She may be hesitant to express her concerns because:

A. She may be afraid of how defensive he may become.
B. She may be worried about how she may react from his aggressive response.

They love each other, but both must recognize they have similar personalities and defensive responses, which may trigger an argument.

This is why before you confront someone, consider the level of your relationship with them before you do anything. Addressing conflict is important, but doing so has a prerequisite of intentionally establishing a relationship. Respect is one of many components of any relationship. If you remove some level of respect, the relationship will be unhealthy and difficult to maintain. If you determine your personalities don't mesh for a relationship to develop, concentrate on establishing mutual respect BEFORE you confront an issue.

In chapter 6, I spoke about how I addressed a co-worker who was demeaning and caused division among my team. Even though I addressed my issues with her, she never changed. My problem was after I decided not to pursue a healthy work relationship with her, I immediately attempted to confront her instead of intentionally establishing mutual respect. She wasn't bothered or concerned by my confrontation because (A) we had no relationship and (B) she didn't respect me. Before you confront the problems of others, purposely pursue a relationship. When you confront someone, it's important that they trust you so that they understand your motives. If someone respects you, they will listen to you even if they don't like you. Remember the couple I spoke about who were unmarried but living together? The reason why he responded positively after I confronted him is because a relationship was established between us. He understood my motives and thanked me in the end for voicing my concerns.

Accountability is so important because there are times when we need someone to confront our issues and help rescue us from our reckless behaviors. Doing this is not judgment but someone awakening us so that we can see the harsh realities we choose to live in. Some of us have been spiritually dead in areas for years because we refuse to allow someone to expose our sin(s). Many of these people are suffering while serving in organizations. Exposing sin will release truth, and this is what can set us free!

KEY POINTS

- Some churches confuse the usage of grace when they should be removing people from ministry who are involved in (willful) sin.

- If a person struggles in an area but does not make consistent efforts to correct their behavior, their actions show they are choosing to live defeated. Grace is unlimited, but God judges based on your intentions for making changes.

- With accountability, we must remember to operate with grace. You restoring someone back to life should outweigh your critique of them.

- When we pretend sin is not present, we are condoning the behavior.

- Accountability is so important because there are times when we need someone to confront our issues and help rescue us from our reckless behavior.

112

CHAPTER 12

WRONG LEADERSHIP

> Then the Lord told him, "I have certainly seen the oppression of my people in Egypt. I have heard their cries of distress because of their harsh slave drivers. Yes, I am aware of their *suffering*." (EXODUS 3:7, NEW LIVING TRANSLATION, EMPHASIS ADDED)

Many of us, either in our professional lives or involvement in ministry, may have experienced being mismanaged and suffer greatly from it. The psychological effects from this can be damaging, ruining confidence and the ability to further develop. Egypt was so traumatizing for the children of Israel that they resisted the bountiful blessings God wanted them to receive. Despite witnessing the Red Sea split, and the Lord moving before them as a cloud by day and a pillar of fire by night, they were indoctrinated to slavery and wanted to return to it.

Like the children of Israel, many of us have witnessed the miraculous performed by God in our lives, yet we doubt and complain to Him when encountering obstacles while in our pursuit to our "promise." We want to return back to our Egypt, which is filled with abuse from leadership, essentially never living out our purpose. God wants us free from wrong leadership, which separates us from accomplishing God's purposes in our lives.

In order to become free from wrong leadership, it's important to correctly identify it. Some of us are quick to label those we may not get along with or those who challenge us to better ourselves as wrong when in fact, they're who God intended to help develop us. It needs to be mentioned that neither this nor any other chapter in this book is intended to serve as making excuses for not submitting to those in authority!

> Obey your leaders and submit to them, for they are keeping watch over your souls, as those who will have to give an account. Let them do this with joy and not with groaning, for that would be of no advantage to you. **(HEBREWS 13:17, ENGLISH STANDARD VERSION)**

This scripture is often taught and used manipulatively to shut the voice of volunteers. Don't misinterpret my position: It's vital and biblical to submit to those in leadership, BUT the writer in verse seven establishes conditions on who to follow.

> Appreciate your pastoral leaders who gave you the Word of God. Take a good look at the way they live, and let their faithfulness instruct you, as well as their truthfulness. There should be a consistency that runs through us all. **(HEBREWS 13:7, THE MESSAGE)**

If there is a lack of and/or questionable faithfulness, truthfulness, and consistency with a leader, we should listen to the voice of God concerning that individual's position in our lives. This is very important because who you give permission to lead you could negatively affect you in various ways. Not only should there be consistency with them, but also with you.

We must understand the correct concept of submission and be led the way God intended. Until Jesus comes back, there will be no perfect ministry or church. Unfortunately, there are leaders who abuse and manipulate, causing emotional harm and separation towards individuals and their families. We must be able to properly identify "right" from "wrong" leadership.

There are many examples in the Bible of great leaders. When reading about these leaders, you will notice a distinction between leading versus managing. It's easy to confuse the two because many professionals use the terms interchangeably when there are distinctions between the two. Management is simply making something or people work. Leadership is significantly broader because it involves building people to become better. In order to build people, one must possess creativity and boldness to motivate and inspire people.

The focus isn't solely based on getting people to do what you want them to do, but building them so that they develop better skills. Leadership looks beyond the present. It prepares the organization and

115

its staff for the future. Correct leadership is unselfish. Many leaders possess different styles, but they all should have the thinking, "I want my people to be better than me." They should desire and train others to think better and execute as this will produce more qualified people to function and serve in our complex world.

116

People who **use their leadership incorrectly** will, at some point, **desire to sabotage** those next in line to assume their position (or a higher position).

> As they were coming home, when David returned from striking down the Philistine, the women came out of all the cities of Israel, singing and dancing, to meet King Saul, with tambourines, with songs of joy, and with musical instruments. And the women sang to one another as they celebrated, "Saul has struck down his thousands, and David his ten thousands." And Saul was very angry, and this saying displeased him. He said, "They have ascribed to David ten thousands, and to me they have ascribed thousands, and what more can he have but the kingdom?" And Saul eyed David from that day on.
> **(1 SAMUEL 18:6-9, ENGLISH STANDARD VERSION)**

118

Probably the most uncomfortable situation for anyone is when his or her leader is jealous, intimidated, or insecure. David dealt with this prior to his rule over Israel. It became so bad that despite his boldness with killing bears, lions, his most famous defeat of Goliath, and other opposing armies, David ran for his life as Saul pursued him because of his jealousy and hatred toward him. Some argue David wasn't afraid of Saul; but despite everything, David respected Saul's authority and the protocol that came with being a King enough not to kill him, even when presented with the opportunity.

> There was a cave there and Saul went in to relieve himself. David and his men were huddled far back in the same cave. David's men whispered to him, "Can you believe it? This is the day God was talking

> about when he said, 'I'll put your enemy in your
> hands. You can do whatever you want with him.'"
> Quiet as a cat, David crept up and cut off a piece
> of Saul's royal robe. (**1 SAMUEL 24:3-4, THE MESSAGE**)

David regarded Saul as his Master and "anointed of the Lord" (1 Samuel 24:6) and would not play any part in his demise even though Saul was out to kill him.

People who use their leadership incorrectly will, at some point, desire to sabotage those next in line to assume their position (or a higher position). Despite Saul being the King, David was more respected, talented, and liked by those Saul ruled over and this infuriated him. This is a trait of wrong leadership. Leaders with correct motives should want others to be better than them. Leadership is unselfish and the intent should be to develop people for the organization's future.

Whether it is the praise and worship leader, the prayer warrior, or even the pastor, there are some today who operate with similar traits as King Saul – which, of course, is wrong for leadership. The following is a list of traits Saul and some leaders today possess, which go against Godly character.

Characteristics	Description	Scripture Support
Insecurity	This is when leaders dominate and intimidate to hide their insecurities. They always find fault but rarely compliment.	Saul wanted to kill David because of his jealousy and hatred toward him (1 Samuel 18:6-9).
Evil Intentions	This is when an individual serves a leader and/or ministry with pure intentions, but is treated poorly in return	David served Saul with good intentions, yet Saul was out to kill him (1 Samuel 18:26-27).
Inflicts Emotional Abuse	This is when leaders deceive people and do not keep their word.	Saul informed David he would allow him to marry his daughter Merab, but later changed his mind and married her to another man (1 Samuel 18:19).

Spirit of Saul

Whether in ministry or any profession, it's important to understand signs of poor leadership, especially when you're the one required to serve. If you encounter circumstances that require you to serve wrong leadership, there is purpose behind it. God still requires us to honor those in authority but he gives us the obligation to act in His character because this is the key to our freedom.

We must use wisdom to counteract the effects of wrong leaderships so that it does not prevent us from accomplishing God's purpose in our lives. If David acted out of character towards Saul, this likely would have jeopardized him from becoming King of Israel.

King Saul had opportunities to accept David's influence and gifts, but he allowed his personal issues to get in the way, which cost him his position as King. Sadly, when he finally recognized David's pure intentions, and was ready to receive him, it was too late – God had already promoted David. Saul was his stepping-stone and even though his intentions were to kill David, God acted on David's behalf.

There are many "Sauls" today who rule over corporations and ministry organizations. God wants to replace these individuals with those with pure intentions and Godly character! Let the "Saul" you face be your stepping-stone. Allow God to use you to relinquish Saul's authority and put it in the hands of a correct leader. Is it you? Are you David?

KEY POINTS

- Neither this nor any other chapter in this book is intended to serve as making excuses for not submitting to those in authority!

- If there is a lack of and/or questionable faithfulness, truthfulness, and consistency with a leader, we should listen to the voice of God concerning that individual's position in our life. This is very important because who you give permission to lead you could negatively affect you in various ways.

- Leadership involves building people to become better. In order to build people, one must possess creativity and boldness to motivate and inspire people.

- Leaders with correct motives should want others to be better than them. Leadership is unselfish and the intent should be to develop people for the organization's future.

- God still requires us to honor those in authority but we are obligated to act in His character because this is the key to our freedom.

CHAPTER 13

SUFFERING = WINNING

Following Jesus will not exempt you from all troubles and sufferings. Yes, there are tremendous benefits that come with salvation, but part of pursuing Christ is the fulfillment of His purpose for your life. The Kingdom benefits greatly when His purpose for your life connects with your willingness to surrender. Once this happens, the world will benefit. Jesus's willingness to surrender His life provided a remedy for sin. Mankind can benefit from this if Jesus is received and lifestyles are changed from pursuing flesh (death) to pursuing life with Jesus!

When Jesus surrendered His life, it came with significant suffering, but this was the ultimate purpose for His life. The fulfillment of purpose comes with suffering because of opposition, which attempts to disrupt and rob mankind from God's grace. This brings us to you and me. How we endure opposition when serving correlates to how we can make a difference and impact societies.

123

There's more to come: We continue to shout our praise even when we're hemmed in with troubles, because we know how troubles can develop passionate patience in us, and how that patience

in turn forges the tempered steel of virtue, keeping us alert for whatever God will do next. In alert expectancy such as this, we're never left feeling shortchanged. Quite the contrary – we can't round up enough containers to hold everything God generously pours into our lives through the Holy Spirit!
(ROMANS 5:3-5, THE MESSAGE)

The world is filled with darkness and when we serve, we have the opportunity to release truth and light. Some of us are serving in darkness. We are the salt God wants to bring to purify His church and the world. A consequence of this is persecution, but God counters it with blessings.

You're blessed when your commitment to God provokes persecution. The persecution drives you even deeper into God's kingdom. **(MATTHEW 5:10, THE MESSAGE)**

124

As believers and followers of Jesus, our intentions should be to stand out, looking different than the world. Influence and real change should come from believers! Just as Jesus impacted the earth, we are to do so in greater measures. Jesus suffered, but He won in the end. When life becomes difficult and when it appears the church is causing more issues in your home-life, expect God to breakout in your circumstances! God may allow hard situations in your life to develop maturity and this process may require suffering. Our loving heavenly Father does not want us abused, manipulated, or our issues neglected. He can

bring us out of these situations if we open ourselves to receive His exit strategy, which may be quick or may be a long turnaround. No matter the duration, He wants issues addressed in the manner pleasing to Him so that you can come out victorious!

Everyone's journey is different, which is why our relationship with Him – listening to His voice and following instructions – is necessary. Suffering is a part of our journey with Jesus, but it shouldn't outweigh the victories we gain as Champions!

> For God is not unrighteous to forget *or* overlook your labor and the love which you have shown for His name's sake in ministering to the needs of the saints (His own consecrated people), as you still do. **(HEBREWS 6:10, AMPLIFIED)**

125

Even if it appears the bad outweighs the good, don't think for a second Almighty God is "suckering" or "pimping" you, abandoning you as you suffer while serving. This is deception at best and this verse explains that to overlook labor is unrighteous – which cannot be a trait of God. Suffering produces the endurance we need to cultivate our character and determine our outcome. When you suffer, you can win.

> The righteous person faces many troubles, but the Lord comes to the rescue each time. For the Lord protects the bones of the righteous; not one of them is broken! **(PSALM 34:19-20, NEW LIVING TRANSLATION)**

REFERENCES

Brennan, W. (2001). HAVING WORDS: Verbal abuse in the workplace. *The Safety & Health Practitioner*, 19(10), 36-38. Retrieved August 9, 2013.

Jacobs, J. L. (2005). *The employee's experience of workplace violence : An exploratory study of the relationship of workplace violence and post-traumatic stress disorder.* (Doctoral dissertation). Retrieved from Union Institute and University, ProQuest, UMI Dissertations Publishing, (Order No. 3172947)

Wilson, I., & Madsen, S. (2008). The Influence of Maslow's Humanistic Views on an Employee's Motivation to Learn. *Journal of Applied Management and Entrepreneurship*, 13(2), 46-62. Retrieved October 25, 2008.

www.ingramcontent.com/pod-product-compliance
Lightning Source LLC
Chambersburg PA
CBHW052109090426
42741CB00009B/1737